THOUGHTS AND SAYINGS

OF

ST. MARGARET MARY

"... thou shalt possess the treasures of My Heart ... and I will permit thee to distribute them as thou wilt, in favor of souls that are ready to receive them."

—Words of Our Lord
to St. Margaret Mary

Saint Margaret Mary Alacoque
1647-1690
Nun of the Order of the Visitation
of Holy Mary

THOUGHTS AND SAYINGS

OF

ST. MARGARET MARY

For Every Day Of The Year

Compiled by
The Sisters of the Visitation
of Paray-le-Monial

Translated by
The Sisters of the Visitation
of Partridge Green, Horsham, West Sussex
(formerly of Roselands, Walmer, Kent)

"Thou must not keep these graces to thyself, nor be sparing in distributing them to others, for I have willed to use thy heart as a channel for conveying them into souls according to My designs; by this means many will be saved from the abyss of perdition."

—Words of Our Lord
to St. Margaret Mary

TAN BOOKS AND PUBLISHERS, INC.
Rockford, Illinois 61105

Nihil Obstat: Michael L. Dempsey, S.T.D.,
                  Censor Theol. Deput.

Imprimatur: ☩ Eduardus,
                  Archiep. Dublinen.,
                  Hibernia Primas
                  Dublini, die 13 Martii, anno 1935

First published in 1935 by the Sisters of the Visitation, Roselands; reprinted by the same in June, 1954. Retypeset and republished in 1986 by TAN Books and Publishers, Inc., by permission of the Sisters of the Visitation, Partridge Green, Horsham, West Sussex, England (formerly of Roselands, Walmer, Kent).

The extracts given in this book have been taken from the 3-volume *Vie et Oeuvres de Sainte Marguerite Marie,* 1920 edition.

Library of Congress Catalog Card No.: 86-50852

ISBN: 0-89555-302-3

Printed and bound in the United States of America.

TAN BOOKS AND PUBLISHERS, INC.
P.O. Box 424
Rockford, Illinois 61105

1986

"I constitute thee heiress of My Heart and of all Its treasures, for time and for eternity, allowing thee to dispose of them according to thy desire; and I promise thee that My assistance will not fail thee as long as My Heart fails not in power. Thou shalt be forever Its beloved disciple."

—Words of Our Lord
to St. Margaret Mary

CONTENTS

VIVE ✠ JESUS!

FOREWORD

Sᴛ. Mᴀʀɢᴀʀᴇᴛ Mᴀʀʏ never had any other Master than her Lord and God, Whom with the greatest love and reverence she called "my Sovereign." Not only did she listen to and meditate on the lessons that He gave her, but she also put them into practice. That is why she was perpetually— even at times simultaneously—drawn to extraordinary heights and depths. "Abyss calleth on abyss." True, such heights and depths are not for everyone. Nevertheless, many souls may derive great spiritual profit from meditating on what the Sacred Heart of Jesus taught His beloved disciple. This opinion has led us to present the reader with selected passages from the instructions our Lord gave the Saint for her personal direction. It will be seen with what solid spiritual food He nourished her soul, and how, by the firm molding of her inner powers, He made her perfectly supple in His adorable hand. Thus He could use her as He pleased for His great and loving designs, and could confide to her an unparalleled mission in His Church. Let us listen to the following words: "My divine Heart is so inflamed with love for men, and for thee in particular that, being unable to contain within Itself the flames of Its burning

Charity, It must needs spread them abroad by thy means." (II, 70).

St. Margaret Mary dedicated and sacrificed herself wholly to the work her divine Master had given her to do, and performed it in the spirit that He had pointed out to her in the following words: "In imitation of Me, and without any other interest than the glory of God, thou must act and suffer in silence, for the establishment of the reign of My Sacred Heart in the hearts of men, to whom I wish to reveal It by thy means." (II, 87).

This insistence of the divine Heart of Jesus, in declaring that He wished to communicate Himself to souls by means of His chosen disciple, is a great consolation to those who enter into supernatural contact with the Saint.

In the second part of this booklet, the reader will find an echo of the preliminary pages — words addressed by our Lord to St. Margaret Mary. The Saint always reverted to the Source whence she had drawn her own spiritual life, viz., to the teaching of that sovereign Master Whose voice vibrated unceasingly within her; therefore, when she is asked for advice, she, of necessity, communicates to the souls of others something of what she herself has heard. Moreover, there is nothing that savors of exaggeration in the advice that she gives. Her words are simple and true, prudent but energetic. Guided by the Holy Spirit she remains faithful to that sound, traditional doctrine which founds the basis of all sanctity upon the hatred of sin and the shunning of willful faults, before making any attempt to rise to the perfection of divine love. But, knowing the cost to nature of the constant struggle needful to be detached from creatures, die to self, embrace the Will of God and accept sufferings and crosses, St. Margaret Mary lights up this rugged path with the vivifying rays emanating from the Sacred Heart. May many souls experience this consolation.

FROM OUR MONASTERY OF
PARAY-LE-MONIAL

JULY 22, 1929
282ND ANNIVERSARY OF THE
BIRTH OF ST. MARGARET MARY

GOD BE PRAISED!
DIEU SOIT BENI!

VIVE ✠ JESUS!

TRANSLATOR'S PREFACE

THIS booklet has been compiled from the *Life and Writings of St. Margaret Mary* with a view to making the Saint better known. Most clients of the Sacred Heart are more or less familiar with our Saint, whom our Lord Himself constituted "Heiress of His Heart and of all Its treasures" (*Life and Writings*, I, 173), but many have not free access to her writings, nor perhaps leisure to study them closely.

The extracts which follow are preceded by quotations from the words of our Lord to the Saint, and have been carefully classified and suitably arranged for the different months of the year.

The writings of St. Margaret Mary, impregnated as they are with implicit trust in the Sacred Heart, cannot fail to be a source of encouragement to souls. From her earliest childhood our Lord became the sole Master and Director of her spiritual life; referring on one occasion to the graces with which He had loaded her, He said, "Thou must not keep these graces to thyself, nor be sparing in distributing them to others, for I have willed to use thy heart as a channel for conveying them into souls according to My designs." (*Life and Writings*, II, 35). St. Margaret Mary ever insisted on the salutary and sanctifying effects of devotion to the Sacred Heart of Jesus, and frequently repeated these words: "Remember that your perfection consists wholly in conforming your life and actions to the sacred maxims of the Heart of Jesus, especially to His patience, His meekness, His humility, and His charity." (II, 667). This should be an incentive to all to read and follow the spiritual counsels given by St. Margaret Mary.

The life-long and ardent wish of our Saint was to see the Kingdom of Christ established in all hearts, and on one occasion she wrote: "I can hardly express my joy at seeing the increase of devotion to the Sacred Heart of my Saviour. I seem to live for that alone. Sometimes such an ardent desire to make It reign in all hearts is kindled within me, that there is nothing I would not do or suffer to bring this about." (II, 304).

We read in her life that she had to suffer much to establish the devotion to the Sacred Heart and, amid the difficulties that beset her, our Lord vouchsafed to encourage her by these words: "Fear nothing, I will reign in spite of My enemies and of all those who would oppose Me." (II, 105), and again: "I will that thou shouldst serve Me as an instrument to draw hearts to My love." (II, 193).

The devotions in honor of the Sacred Heart on the First Friday of the month, now almost universal, are a striking proof that St. Margaret Mary has been instrumental in drawing innumerable hearts to the love and worship of the Heart of her divine Master.

Another devotion, which in recent years has become so widespread, is that of the "holy hour." At the express command of our Lord Himself, St. Margaret Mary was the first to spend an hour in union with the sorrowful prayer He willed to make in the Garden of Gethsemani. This devotion is a source of great graces to souls, drawing them, as it does, into close contact with the agonizing and loving Heart of our Saviour, and being a direct response to His plaintive appeal: "Could you not watch one hour with Me?"

The promise that our divine Saviour made to His faithful spouse, that He would reign in spite of all who opposed Him, is in the present time being fulfilled by the "Enthronement of the Sacred Heart in the Home," for as Pius XI says in his encyclical *Quas Primas*, "This pious custom, practiced by innumerable families, of dedicating and surrendering themselves to the Sacred Heart of Jesus, is an acknowledgment of the Kingship and sovereign rule of Christ."

Finally, the establishment in the Church of the Feast of the Kingship of Christ has verily extended the reign of the Heart of Jesus to the ends of the world, and is the response of the Church, His Kingdom on earth, to the impious and rebellious cry of an atheistical, self-worshipping world: "We will not have this man to reign over us!" (*Luke* 19:14).

As the sovereign rule of Christ over society is

to be brought about only by the personal holiness of each member of that society, we cannot do better than turn to the apostle and disciple of His Sacred Heart, to learn from her how to conform our lives to the teachings of her divine Master. Animated by her ardent desire to see the Sacred Heart reign over all hearts, we shall say in the words of St. Pius X: "O divine King, we desire that Thou be Master of all. We acknowledge and publicly proclaim Thy sovereign dominion and Thy absolute right to reign. We acknowledge and publicly proclaim Thy rights over society, and we desire that they be solemnly recognized by the whole world."

FEAST OF CHRIST THE KING, 1934.

DIEU SOIT BENI!

WORDS ADDRESSED BY OUR LORD
TO ST. MARGARET MARY

BEFORE quoting any of our Lord's words, it may be well to make an observation.

Owing to the extreme violence St. Margaret Mary had been obliged to do herself, to begin writing her life through obedience, she complained to our Lord Himself and, among other things, alleged the difficulty of remembering what had happened more than twenty-five years ago. The divine Master replied: "Dost thou not know that I am the eternal memory of My heavenly Father, by Whom nothing is forgotten, and before Whom the past and the future are as the present? Write, therefore, without fear, according as I shall dictate to thee, and I promise thee the unction of My grace in order that I may be thereby glorified."   II, 35.

Could a more authentic proof be desired of the truth of the words first heard and then written by the humble Saint? We shall doubtless discover that our Lord has impregnated them with the "unction of His grace."

My divine Master once gave me the following lesson: "Learn that I am a holy Master, and One that teaches holiness, I am pure, and cannot endure the slightest stain. Therefore thou must act in My presence with simplicity of heart and with an upright and pure intention. Know that I cannot endure the least want of straightforwardness, and I shall make thee understand that, if the excess of My love has led Me to constitute Myself thy Master, in order to teach and fashion thee after My manner and according to My designs, nevertheless I cannot bear tepid and cowardly souls. If I am gentle in bearing with thy weakness, I shall not be less severe and exact in correcting and punishing thy infidelities."   II, 67.

"If thou remainest faithful to Me, I will never forsake thee . . . I forgive thy ignorance, because, as yet, thou dost not know Me; but, if thou art faithful to Me and followest Me, I will teach thee to know Me, and I will reveal Myself to thee."

II, 47.

"See, My daughter, whether thou canst find a father whose love for his only son has prompted him to take such care of him or to show him such tender proofs of his love as I have given and will yet give thee of Mine; for from thy earliest years My love has borne kindly with thee, and has trained and formed thee after My own Heart, awaiting thee patiently without growing weary of all thy resistance. Know, therefore, that if ever thou shouldst forget the gratitude thou owest Me and shouldst not refer the glory of everything to Me, thou wouldst thereby, as regards thyself, dry up this inexhaustible source of all good." II, 55.

"I will make thee understand that I am a wise and learned director, Who will safely lead those souls who, forgetful of themselves, abandon themselves to Me." II, 69.

"Consider what thou art and what thou deservest, and then wilt thou understand whence comes the good which is in thee. Why dost thou fear, since I have given thee that place of refuge in which all things are made easy?" II, 133.

"Acknowledge that without Me thou canst do nothing, but I will never let thee lack help as long as thou keepest thy weakness and nothingness buried in My strength." II, 59.

"Let Me do everything in its own time, for at present I will have thee to be the sport of My love, which will treat thee according to its good pleasure." II, 62.

"Be ever ready and disposed to receive Me, because henceforth I will make My abode in thee so as to hold familiar converse with thee." II, 62.

"Listen, My daughter, believe not lightly and trust not every spirit, for Satan is enraged and will seek to deceive thee. Therefore, do nothing without the approval of those who guide thee; if thou art thus under the authority of obedience, his efforts against thee will be in vain, for he has no power over the obedient."   II, 73.

"Not only do I desire that thou shouldst do what thy Superiors command, but also that thou shouldst do nothing of all that I order thee without their consent. I love obedience, and without it no one can please Me."   II, 65.

"Learn that the more thou retirest into thy nothingness, the more My greatness stoops to find thee."   II, 139.

"I will give thee My Heart, but thou must first constitute thyself Its holocaust."   II, 84.

"I desire to make of thee an example of My combined Love and Mercy."   II, 46.

"I have chosen thee as an abyss of unworthiness and ignorance for the accomplishment of this great design, so that everything may be done by Me."   II, 70.

"Alas, my God, I know my weakness, I fear to betray Thee, and that with me Thy gifts may not be in safe keeping." "Fear nothing, My daughter," He replied, "I shall see to everything, for I constitute Myself the Guardian of My gifts and will render thee powerless to resist Me." II, 65.

"Never forget that thou art a mere nothing and, being the victim of My Heart, thou must always be ready to be immolated in the cause of charity. For this reason My love will not be inactive within thee, but will always make thee act or suffer without thy being able to lay the least claim to anything as thy due, any more than a piece of work belongs to the tool used by the artisan."

II, 193.

"I will make thee appear so poor, so vile and so abject in thine own eyes, and will so completely annihilate thee in thine own opinion, that I may be able to build up Mine own Self upon this nothingness." II, 364.

"Remember that it is a crucified God Whom thou wilt espouse, therefore thou must make thyself conformable to Him, and bid farewell to all the pleasures of life, since there will no longer be any for thee but such as are marked with the cross." II, 139.

"Behold the wound in My Side where thou art to make thy dwelling now and forever. There wilt thou be able to preserve the robe of innocence with which I have clothed thy soul, so that thou mayest henceforth live the life of a Man-God, living as no longer living, that I may live perfectly in thee. . . . To do this, if thou dost not wish to outrage My omnipotence and grievously offend Me, thy powers and senses must remain buried in Me ... seeking nothing apart from Me, since I wish to be all things to thee."   II, 190.

"I, Who govern thee, am He to Whom thou must be wholly abandoned, without any care or thought of thyself, since My help will only fail thee when My Heart fails in power."   II, 194.

"What hast thou to fear in the arms of the Almighty? Could I possibly allow thee to perish and deliver thee up to thy enemies, after having constituted Myself thy Father, thy Master and thy Ruler from thy earliest years and given thee continual proofs of the loving tenderness of My Heart?"   II, 90.

"What, am I not sufficient for thee, I Who am thy beginning and thy last end?"   II, 194.

"If I wish thee to be deaf, dumb and blind in My presence, must thou not be content to be so?"   II, 129.

"I have chosen thy soul to be a paradise of rest to Me on earth, and thy heart shall be a throne of delight for My divine love."   I, 266.

"What hast thou to boast of, O dust and ashes, since of thyself thou art nought but nothingness and misery; thou shouldst never lose sight thereof and shouldst ever remain buried in this abyss of thy nothingness. Lest the greatness of My gifts lead thee to forget what thou art, behold I will set before thee this portrait of thyself."

II, 76.

"Lose thyself in My immensity and see that thou never depart therefrom. For shouldst thou do so, thou wilt never again obtain admittance."

II, 131.

"I have yet a rough and heavy cross to place upon thy weak shoulders; but I am powerful enough to sustain it; fear nothing, and let Me do with thee and in thee whatsoever I will." II, 194.

"What dost thou fear, since I have answered for thee and made Myself thy surety?"   II, 203.

"If, hitherto, thou hast taken only the name of My slave, I now give thee that of the beloved disciple of My Sacred Heart."   II, 71.

"I will give thee to read in the Book of Life which contains the science of love." And revealing to me His Sacred Heart, He made me read in It the following words: "My love reigns in suffering, it triumphs in humility and rejoices in unity."

II, 152.

"Thou hast still a long, painful and rugged path to tread, on which thou wilt often need to take breath and rest in My Sacred Heart; on that account It shall always be open to thee, as long as thou walkest in Its ways." II, 193.

"Behold how sinners treat Me ... My daughter, wilt thou give Me thy heart and ease My suffering love which everyone despises?" II, 152, 145.

"I wish thy heart to serve Me as a refuge wherein I may withdraw and take My delight when sinners persecute and drive Me from theirs." II, 193.

"Be ever ready to receive Me, for I shall always be ready to give Myself to thee. Thou wilt often be given over to the fury of thy enemies, but, fear nothing; I will surround thee with My power, and will Myself be the reward of thy victories. Be careful never to look at thyself apart from Me. Let thy motto be: 'To love and suffer blindly. One only heart, one only love, one God alone.'" II, 190.

"Fear nothing and trust in Me. I am thy Protector and thy Surety. Within thy soul I have established My reign of peace which no one shall disturb, and in thy heart My reign of love which will fill thee with joy; of this joy no one shall deprive thee." II, 194.

"I desire that thou mayest serve Me as an instrument to draw hearts to My love." II, 193.

"Dost thou know why I give thee My graces in such abundance? To make of thee a sanctuary in which the fire of My love may continually burn. Thy heart is like a sacred altar which nothing sullied may touch; I have chosen it as an altar of holocausts for My Eternal Father." II, 145.

"I will remember those who have confidence in thy prayers, so that thou mayest be entirely occupied and taken up with My love." II, 194.

"Abandon everything to My good pleasure and let Me accomplish My designs; do not thou interfere in anything, for I will have care of all." II, 91.

One day, as I was yearning to receive our Lord, I said to Him: "Teach me what Thou wouldst have me to say to thee." "Nothing but these words: 'My God, my only Good and my All, Thou art wholly mine, and I am wholly Thine.' They will preserve thee from all kinds of temptations, will supply for all the acts thou wouldst make, and serve as preparation for all thy actions." II, 167.

"I have heard thy sighs, and the desires of thy heart are so pleasing to Me, that had I not instituted My divine Sacrament of love, I would do so now for love of thee, so as to have the pleasure of dwelling in thy soul and of taking My loving repose in thy heart." II, 106.

"I constitute thee heiress of My Heart and of all Its treasures, for time and for eternity, allowing thee to dispose of them according to thy desire; and I promise thee that My assistance will not fail thee, as long as My Heart fails not in power. Thou shalt be forever Its beloved disciple."   I, 173.

When I placed before Him my humble petitions regarding those things that it seems difficult to obtain [concerning the devotion to the Sacred Heart], I seemed to hear these words: "Dost thou believe that I can do this? If thou dost believe thou shalt behold the omnipotence of My Heart in the magnificence of My love."

As I watch its steady progress I hear those other words: "Did I not indeed tell thee, that if thou couldst believe, thou shouldst see thy desires accomplished?"   II, 429.

THOUGHTS AND SAYINGS
OF
ST. MARGARET MARY

JANUARY

The Practice of Virtue

1

If you are faithful to do the Will of God in time, yours shall be accomplished throughout eternity.   II, 747.

2

You know that there is no middle course, and that it is a question of being saved or lost for all eternity. It depends on us: either we may choose to love God eternally with the Saints in Heaven after we have done violence to self here below by mortifying and crucifying ourselves as they did, or else renounce their happiness by giving to nature all for which it craves.   II, 374.

3

If you wish to regain the good graces of our Lord Jesus Christ, you must no longer commit any voluntary fault, otherwise, you will seek for them in vain.   II, 371.

4

What punishment will not that servant bring upon himself who knows the will of his Master and does not do it?   II, 502.

5

This strong insistence of grace that you feel amidst so many relapses is, to my mind, a very good sign, because it shows the ardent desire that God has to save your soul; this, nevertheless, He will not do without your cooperation.   II, 371.

6

It is only necessary to say energetically "I will," and all will go well.   II, 372.

7

I think you would please our Lord by going to Him with the dispositions of the prodigal son, in such wise that fear may not banish confidence. It is not said, however, that this son, after having returned to his father, left him a second time.

II, 372.

8

Our Lord is satisfied with our good will. I hope that His Heart will never refuse you the graces necessary to fulfill entirely all that He requires of you.   II, 263.

9

It seems to me we have nothing to fear when we look to God only and seek His glory alone; since He takes into account the good will alone of a heart that loves Him.   II, 258.

10

Our self-love is so subtle; at times it makes us believe that we are seeking God, because we are so much attached to the things of His service, that we feel some annoyance when obliged to leave them. This is because we seek our own satisfaction rather than God; a heart that wishes for Him alone, finds Him everywhere.   II, 686.

11

Great graces are often attached to what seems trifling.   II, 662.

12

Virtue does not consist in making good resolutions, nor in saying fine words, but in keeping one's resolutions and carrying out one's good intentions.   II, 660.

13

Our falls are the result of the continual revolt of our passions. But we need not be troubled, cast down or discouraged by them: we must do violence to ourselves and draw profit from them.
                                                        II, 389.

14

Let us begin in earnest to work out our salvation, for no one will do it for us, since even He Himself, Who made us without ourselves, will not save us without ourselves.   II, 502.

15

Let us profit by the time which He gives us and delay no longer; but let us not be anxious, for anxiety serves but to increase our trouble. II, 373.

16

Since God wishes it—there is nothing to be done. . . . Why should you thus torment yourself? Get rid of whatever He shows you to be an obstacle to His love, for His only desire is that you should live stripped of all that is not Himself.

II, 681.

17

When there is a question of salvation, we must do and suffer everything, sacrifice and give up everything.   II, 495.

18

Go courageously to God, along the way He has traced out for you, steadfastly embracing the means He offers you.   II, 375.

19

By wishing to do too much, we often spoil everything, constraining our Lord to leave us to act alone and withdraw from us in sorrow. II, 473.

20

Let us not waste time reflecting so much upon our troubles, either past or present. We must think about them as little as possible, for they have less power to harm us when we disregard and ignore them.   II, 682.

21

You must be indifferent to all created things and especially to the impulses prompted by your self-love and your own will. This self-will He wishes you to sacrifice as often as He gives you the opportunity thereof, by breaking and thwarting it, until it is wholly destroyed and extinct, in order that the Will of His divine Heart, alone, may reign in you.   II, 694.

22

You know what you have to do. Correspond faithfully, joyfully and willingly to the lights He gives you.   II, 671.

23

Nature and grace cannot subsist together in the same heart. The one must always make room for the other.   II, 374.

24

Do not deceive yourself, you will obtain nothing except at the very point of the sword. That is to say, you must do violence to self, and be of the number of those who take Heaven by storm.   II, 674.

25

I beg of Him with all my heart to make you

ever faithful to what He asks of you, ready to sacrifice to Him all that costs you the most, according as He makes His Will known to you; for there is no middle course; He will have all or nothing. II, 373.

26

Forget your own interests and leave the care of yourself to your heavenly Father. The further you withdraw from self, the closer you draw to God. II, 709.

27

Try to draw profit from and make good use of the holy affections that you receive from the Sovereign Goodness, endeavoring to benefit by them. Be ever attentive to good inspirations, for the Holy Spirit breathes where He wills. Grace is offered, but if refused, never returns. Therefore let us profit by it. II, 380.

28

Be faithful to the practice of virtue, never willfully neglecting any occasion thereof. II, 677.

29

When our Lord inspires us with some good deed, He also gives the strength to do it. II, 380.

30

He will take good care to provide what is necessary for our sanctification, provided we are careful to accept everything according to His designs.   II, 441.

31

If you find within yourself an abyss of pride and vain esteem, bury these passions in the abyss of the humility of the Sacred Heart, wherein you must lose all that stirs you interiorly, so as to be arrayed in His sacred annihilations.   II, 754.

FEBRUARY

Patience—Generosity

1

Now is the time to suffer and to fight with humble submission, in order to purify and perfect yourself according to His Will, so that you may be worthy to accomplish His designs regarding you. What have you to fear, since His power surrounds you on all sides like an impregnable wall against the attacks of your enemies. Remember that when God wishes to purify a soul by suffering, no one can console or relieve it.   II, 697.

2

You know that virtue is not practiced without effort, but for one moment of suffering there follows an eternity of reward.   II, 678.

3

Again I say, do not worry over your faults, but when you have committed any, say quite trustfully to the all-loving Heart of Jesus: "O my only Love, pay for Thy poor slave and repair the evil that I have just done."   II, 411.

4

Courage then! Finish what you have begun for

the sake of this divine Heart, and rest assured
that our Lord will repay you a hundredfold for all
that you do for His love.   II, 390.

5

We must never be discouraged or give way to
anxiety ... but ever have recourse to the adorable
Heart of Jesus.   II, 682.

6

This divine Heart is a fortress and a sure refuge
for all who would take shelter therein, to avoid
the strokes of divine Justice.   II, 363.

7

If you are faithful to your promises, He will be
very liberal in His favors. He will give you peace
after your struggles, and unknown to you, will
bring you to the goal He has planned.   II, 712.

8

We cannot be saved without a struggle, for this
life is a continual warfare. But be of good courage,
do not be disheartened or troubled about your
faults, but always try to draw from them a love of
abjection, which must never for a moment be ab-
sent from your heart.   II, 704.

9

O my Saviour, who am I, that Thou shouldst
have so long awaited my repentance!   II, 206.

10

Doubtless you are one of those plants which the Heavenly Father has set in His Garden to cultivate with His own Hand, to preserve by His Providence, to unfold by His grace, and to cause to flower in the odor of sweetness by the warmth of His sacred love, provided that you courageously resist the opposition the enemy will strive to raise.   II, 671.

11

Believe me, do not be cast down or grieved at the small vexations by which it pleases our Lord to try your love and patience; but endeavor rather to conform your will to His, letting Him do with you according to His desire, which is, that you should remain peaceful and resigned in the midst of your difficulties.   II, 680.

12

You can walk in the way that God has traced out for you only by continual self-denial and by renouncing that strong attachment you have for creatures. Die, therefore, to all these useless affections, so that Jesus may live in you.   II, 645.

13

Go forward, forget yourself, and let Him act, for He loves you; by wanting to do too much, you hinder Him from furthering the work of your perfection.   II, 403.

14

It should suffice for us that God is satisfied. I am sure that neither you nor I wish for anything else. Let us then love our Lord, and give Him all without reserve.   II, 233.

15

Look upon yourself as a tree planted beside the water, which bears its fruit in due season; the more it is shaken by the wind, the deeper it strikes its roots into the ground.   II, 677.

16

Keep yourself in the presence of our Lord, not only during prayer, but also at other times, as a disciple before his Master, anxious to do His Will by giving up his own.   II, 707.

17

I think that this fear which our Lord makes you feel is the result of His very great love for you; for seeing that your love for Him is not powerful enough to make you do good and avoid evil, He mingles fear with love, that the two together may make you do what He desires of you.   II, 669.

18

Be of good courage, for neither grace nor the help of the Sacred Heart will be wanting to you. Our Lord wishes to save you; He will not let you

perish so long as you do not willfully do what you
know displeases Him.   II, 674.

19

Seeing that this divine Shepherd has taken so
many steps in seeking you, you will return Him
thanks for it and, uniting all your steps to His, ask
His help to walk henceforth only in the way of
His love. Say often to Him: O my kind Shepherd,
detach me from all earthly things and from
myself, that I may be united to Thee.   II, 723.

20

Be inviolably faithful to Him, whatever it may
cost you, for He is rich enough to reward all.
                                         II, 696.

21

Reflect that this same grace, which prompts
you now so earnestly and which you have so
often resisted, will weaken and lessen by degrees,
and eventually withdraw from you, leaving your
soul like dry and barren soil.... May God preserve you from such a misfortune.   II, 672.

22

He wishes your fidelity to be unswerving.
Whatever it may cost you, you must persevere,
for the Sacred Heart is averse to every sort of inconstancy—and this is your greatest fault; but it
is only you yourself who, with the grace of God,

can remedy it by continually doing violence to
self.   II, 760.

23

I advise you to have recourse to the Sacred
Heart of our Lord Jesus Christ, if you want to
conquer your enemies and obtain the strength
and consolation you need; He will not refuse you
this help, if you ask it of Him.   II, 507.

24

Do nothing through human respect and, when
it assails you, say: I shall do neither more nor less
for the eyes of creatures. O my God, since I wish
to please Thee alone, it suffices that Thou seest
me everywhere.   II, 652.

25

Go courageously to God, along the way He has
traced out for you, steadfastly embracing the
means He offers you.   II, 375.

26

Could you but realize what happiness it is to
love the Sacred Heart of Jesus, you would despise
all else to love but It alone.   II, 678.

27

The crown will be given neither to beginners,
nor to the advanced, but to the victorious, to
those who persevere to the end.   II, 758.

28

Receive not grace in vain, for it is as terrible to fall into the hands of a living God, as it is sweet to cast oneself at present into the arms of a God dying for love of us.   II, 358.

29

If you are submerged in the waters of infidelity and inconstancy, plunge yourself into the fathomless deep of the Sacred Heart. Its stability and steadfastness will teach you to be faithful to Him—our true and faithful Friend—and constant in His service, as He has ever been in His love for us.   II, 754.

MARCH

The Will of God

1

It seems to me that the happiness of a soul consists entirely in conforming to the most adorable Will of God; for in so doing the heart finds peace and the spirit joy and repose, since he "who is joined to the Lord is one spirit" with Him. (*1 Cor.* 6:17). II, 265.

2

I feel so utterly possessed by my divine and loving Master, that I am powerless to have recourse to anyone else in my wants or difficulties, be they great or small....When I feel my strength failing, I call on Him for help, saying: "Thou art my strength and support!" II, 147, 148.

3

Affliction or consolation, health or sickness, is all one to a heart that loves. Since we wish only to please God, it should be enough for us that His Will is accomplished. II, 248.

4

No one can resist the Will of God, which will

always be accomplished whether we will or no.

                                        II, 494.

5

Let us submit to the orders of our Sovereign
Master, and confess that—in spite of all that
seems harsh and distressing—He is good and just
in all He does and that He has a right at all times
to our praise and love.   II, 244.

6

Have no other desire or intention but to please
God in all that you do. See Him alone in everything that befalls you.   II, 708.

7

Take as your motto and aspiration in every
event and frame of mind, these words of our
Lord: "Thy Will be done!" adding: "My God I
abandon myself to Thee."   II, 689.

8

Strive ever to walk in the liberty of the children
of God, conforming and uniting yourself to His
holy love and holy Will; for in His Will you must
die to your own, so as to have but one will with
Him.   II, 666.

9

Give up your own will and submit your judg-
ment whenever you have the opportunity of so

doing, for I think that this is very pleasing to
God.   II, 673.

10

It should be enough for us to follow blindly His
most holy Will.   II, 377.

11

Provided He is satisfied, it suffices. Let Him
act, and let your sole occupation be to love Him,
and your sole aim not to resist Him or put any
obstacle in the way of His designs.   II, 410.

12

When He desired something from me, He
urged me so strongly that it was impossible to
resist.   II, 82.

13

He only asks of you abandonment and perfect
submission. Nothing displeases Him so much as
your uneasiness and despondency. What do you
fear? Is He not powerful enough to support you?
Why, then, are you so reserved with Him? Let
Him act!   II, 713.

14

We must submit to the Will of God and kiss
the hand that strikes us, for we know it is better
to suffer in this life than in the next, since one
moment of suffering willingly accepted for the

love of God, is worth an eternity of happiness.
                                             II, 435.

15

I must no longer concern myself about anything it may please my Sovereign Master to do
with me and in me; He has told me that He will
cease to take care of me only when I am preoc-
cupied with self. I have experienced this many
times through my infidelity, the outcome of
which was the thwarting of my wishes. But I no
longer have any desire but to do what He has told
me many a time: "Leave it to Me to act." II, 251.

16

I was equally pleased whether what I asked for
was granted or refused; provided that I obeyed I
was satisfied.   II, 100.

17

The divine Heart of Jesus must be so entirely
substituted for our own, that He alone may live
and act in us and for us; His Will must so annihilate ours that it may have absolute freedom to act
without any resistance on our part; in fact, His
affections, thoughts and desires must take the
place of ours: thus He will love Himself with His
own love in us and for us.   II, 472.

18

When we give ourselves up entirely to His
guidance and allow Him to do as He pleases with

us, He enables us to make great progress in a short time, almost without our knowing it, except for the struggles in which His grace continually engages our immortified nature.   II, 379.

19

Like a faithful servant, you must forget yourself so as to work wholeheartedly in the service of your divine Master, Who will reward your actions in proportion to your love alone.   II, 733.

20

There is no other remedy for your ills but patience and submission to the Will of God. II, 496.

21

He wishes for humble and submissive hearts that will have no other interest but to accomplish His good pleasure.   II, 532.

22

To work or to suffer is all one to a heart that loves. Let us, then, leave the future to the loving Providence of this divine Heart Which only asks of us fidelity to the present moment.   II, 598.

23

Love Him with all your strength, think always of Him, let Him do with you, in you and for you whatever He wills, and do not be anxious about anything else.   II, 665.

24

Those, who in all simplicity look only to God in what they do, take for their motto: When alone, I will act as when in the sight of creatures, since God sees me everywhere, and He knows the inmost recesses of my heart.   II, 275.

25

Place over the eyes of your soul the bandage of holy and loving submission to God. . . . Thus without reasoning or swerving from your path, go forward on your way.   II, 659.

26

Cling to God, and leave all the rest to Him: He will not let you perish. Your soul is very dear to Him, He wishes to save it.   II, 681.

27

You will obey promptly, simply, lovingly and without replying, to those who have power to command you, remembering these words: "I did not come to do my own will, but the Will of Him Who called me."   II, 747.

28

Refer all events to God and never to creatures—this will enable you to receive from His adorable hand sweetness as well as bitterness, vexations as well as consolations and help you ever to bless Him.   II, 665.

29

Abandon yourself wholly to His adorable Heart, putting aside your own interests, so as to devote yourself exclusively and wholeheartedly to the work He has given you to do; then you will be able to say that His most holy Will has been done in everything He has made known to you.

II, 262.

30

Now is the time of a fruitful sowing for eternity, when the harvest will be plentiful. Do not lose courage. Your sufferings endured with patience are worth a thousand times more than any other austerity. This is what God asks of you for the present.

II, 495.

31

If we find ourselves in an abyss of resistance and opposition to the Will of God, we must submerge it in that of submission and conformity to the divine good pleasure of the Sacred Heart of our Lord. There, losing all our resistance, let us clothe ourselves with that salutary conformity to all His designs in our regard.

II, 753.

APRIL

Peace—Trust—Abandonment

1

May the peace of the adorable Heart of Jesus Christ ever fill our hearts, so that nothing may be able to disturb our serenity!　　　　II, 263.

2

The Spirit of God does all things in peace. Let us have recourse to God with love and confidence, and He will receive us into the arms of His mercy.　　　　II, 373.

3

Bury all your misery in the mercy of the loving Heart of Jesus and think of nothing but of pleasing Him by forgetting self. Henceforth let Him do all that He wills in you, with you and for you.

II, 692.

4

It is His Will that we should apply to Him in all our needs, with humble, respectful, but very filial trust, abandoning ourselves entirely to His loving care like children to a good father.　　　　II, 557.

5

Keep your heart in peace and let nothing trouble you, not even your faults. You must humble yourself and amend them peacefully, without being discouraged or cast down, for God's dwelling is in peace.   II, 653.

6

When you have committed faults, do not be anxious because anxiety, uneasiness and too much agitation withdraw the soul from God and cause Jesus Christ to withdraw from the soul. Let us, rather, ask pardon of Him and beg His Sacred Heart to restore us to favor.   II, 683.

7

Act towards our Lord with entire confidence and simplicity: do not spend time by dwelling too often on your past faults; this only serves to satisfy self-love and to discourage us.   II, 709.

8

Have great confidence in God and never distrust His mercy, which infinitely surpasses all our misery.   II, 673.

9

Hope in His goodness and redouble your confidence in proportion as your troubles increase.
                                        II, 677.

10

Have recourse trustfully to God's loving kindness and He will not forsake you, for He longs to bestow His graces. Though you may have had the misfortune to offend Him, He is always ready to receive you, provided you return humbly to Him.

II, 503.

11

Notwithstanding my weakness, I am no longer afraid; I have placed my confidence in God Who can do all things, and from Whom I hope all things, for I rely not on myself.　　　II, 203.

12

When you are in trouble and anxiety, go and plunge yourself in the peace of this adorable Heart, which no one can take from you.　II, 755.

13

I think you will please the Sacred Heart of our Lord Jesus Christ, if you so completely surrender yourself to Him, that you will see Him alone and hear Him alone, that He alone may illumine your understanding, be the motive power of your will, the abiding thought of your memory and the supreme love of your heart.　　　II, 654.

14

What have you to fear except to lose that confidence in Him, which constrains Him to stoop from the throne of His omnipotence and condescend to come to the aid of our weakness?

II, 443.

15

In everything and everywhere, I desire nothing but the accomplishment of the divine good pleasure, allowing the divine Heart of Jesus to will and desire in me and for me, just as He pleases. I am content to love Him alone: whatever He wishes me to love, that He will love for me.   II, 535.

16

From those whom He loves, Jesus wills to have all without reserve, that is to say, entire conformity of life to His holy maxims, and complete self-effacement, self-forgetfulness and self-surrender, with loving trustfulness, to the care of His Providence.   II, 469.

17

He alone suffices to my heart and my soul, which desire nothing save to rest quite simply in His divine presence, without making any other acts than those of love. It is thus that I frequently spend whole days: they are never long enough to love my God.   II, 137.

18

What joy to belong entirely to God, to make one's dwelling in Him, and to lay in Him the basis of one's perfection! In Him the soul enjoys a

reign of imperturbable peace, where it beholds
the vicissitudes and events of life without being
perturbed or disturbed by them, for they vanish
like a dream; nevertheless, in proportion as we
despise them, the more profitable they will be.

II, 470.

19

Think no more of what people say, but of
pleasing the Heart of Jesus alone, according to the
lights He will give you. He loves you and He will
never allow you to perish, so long as you trust in
Him.   II, 713.

20

As regards your taking up your abode in His
Sacred Heart, why should you fear? Our Lord
Himself invites you to come to Him and take
your rest in His Heart. Is It not the throne of mercy, where the most miserable are the most favora-
bly received, provided that, although steeped in
misery, they are drawn by love?   II, 410.

21

Practice abandonment as regards your body,
taking and accepting indifferently sickness or
health, work or rest—abandonment as regards
your soul, cherishing dryness, insensibility, deso-
lation, and accepting them with the same
thanksgiving as you would sweetness and consolation.   II, 691.

22

Remain in peace, wholly given over and immolated to the Sacred Heart of our Lord Jesus Christ Who, I am sure, will never forsake you. He will take very special care of you, in proportion as you trust in Him, and abandon yourself with unswerving fidelity to Him, whenever there is a question of proving your love.   II, 497.

23

Rely entirely on God with perfect confidence in His goodness, which never forsakes those who, distrusting themselves, hope in Him.   II, 375.

24

Do not be afraid to abandon yourself unreservedly to His loving Providence, for a child cannot perish in the arms of a Father Who is omnipotent.   II, 411.

25

Cast yourself often into His arms or into His divine Heart, and abandon yourself to all His designs upon you.   II, 673.

26

I think our Lord will grant you many graces if you have the courage to follow Him by entire self-forgetfulness, abandonment to His Providence and great purity of intention, always uniting yourself to the intentions of His Sacred Heart.

II, 361.

27

Let us have no further reserve with Him; let us abandon to Him all that we are, without anxiety about the future, not reflecting on ourselves and our incapacity.   II, 423.

28

Keep your soul always in peace, with love and trust in our Lord, and—I repeat—remember what you have promised Him, that is to say, undivided love, persevering humility and generous mortification. This is what you owe to the Sacred Heart of Jesus.   II, 714.

29

Know that He wishes more love than fear from you. Therefore, abandon yourself to His love, and let Him act in you, with you and for you, according to His desire and good pleasure.   II, 483.

30

Should you find yourself overwhelmed by fear, cast yourself into the abyss of the unshaken confidence of the Sacred Heart, and there your fear will give place to love. If you find yourself frail and weak, lapsing into faults at every moment, go to the Sacred Heart and draw from It the strength which will invigorate and revive you.

II, 753, 755.

MAY

Prayer—Union with God

1

I am very glad that our Lord inspires you at prayer to view your misery in the great mercy of the Sacred Heart. Beg of Him earnestly to show His mercy to you and to all sinners.　　II, 680.

2

Choose the divine Heart for your sacred oratory, wherein to offer to God your petitions and prayers that they may be pleasing to Him. II, 362.

3

If you wish to pray well, be faithful in the practice of mortification, avoid dissipation of mind during the day, and never commit any willful faults.　　　　　　　　　　　　　　　II, 714.

4

Everything depends on prayer well made; but in order to pray well, one must be very recollected and mortified.　　　　　　　　　II, 657.

5

You have only to unite yourself in all that you

do to the Sacred Heart of our Lord Jesus Christ. At the beginning of your actions, make His dispositions your own, and at the end offer His merits as satisfaction. For instance you cannot pray: Be satisfied to unite yourself with the prayer our divine Saviour makes for us in the Blessed Sacrament of the Altar, and offer His ardor to make reparation for your lukewarmness. Say before each of your actions: My God I will do or suffer this in the Sacred Heart of Thy divine Son, and according to His most holy intentions, which I offer Thee to atone for all that is imperfect in mine.   II, 498.

6

Now is the time to humble myself and show God that I love Him.   II, 746.

7

We can tell Him all the secrets of our heart, disclosing our want and misery to Him Who alone can remedy them, and saying: O Friend of my heart, she whom Thou lovest is sick. Visit and heal me, for I well know that Thou canst not love me and yet leave me alone in my distress. II, 724.

8

Always maintain interior silence, speaking seldom to creatures, but often to God by your works, suffering and doing all for love of Him.
                                                          II, 695.

9

If you are overwhelmed by sadness, go and plunge your soul into the ocean of the divine joy of the Sacred Heart; there you will discover a treasure that will dispel all your heaviness of heart and dejection of mind.   II, 755.

10

Let us adore and love God through the adorable Heart of Jesus: let us do all our actions in Him; let us beg Him to do all in us and for us, and to restore us to grace by uniting us again to His Father, when sin has separated us from Him.

II, 725.

11

One of the ways most pleasing to God of keeping ourselves in His holy presence, is to enter into the Sacred Heart of Jesus and to commit to Him all the care of ourselves. We must abide therein as in an abyss of love, and lose in it that which is of ourselves, so that He may substitute that which is of Himself.   II, 701.

12

We must keep control over all our senses by holy interior recollection, banishing all useless reflection and introspection; these only serve to disturb us and deprive our soul of that peace without which it will never be the sanctuary of God.   II, 391.

13

My sweet Jesus, I unite my soul to Thy Soul, and my heart, my mind, my life and my intentions to Thine; and, thus united, I present myself to Thy Father. Receive me, O Eternal Father, through the merits of Thy beloved Son.   II, 799.

14

Though Jesus [in His Sacred Humanity] is solitary in the Blessed Sacrament, He is always communing with God. Therefore, in order to be conformed to Him, I will make a solitude in my heart, so that everywhere I may converse alone with Jesus.   II, 741.

15

If you wish to acquire the gift of prayer, you must humbly persevere in mortifying your senses.... I especially advise you to be very faithful to holy recollection, mortifying your eyes, your tongue and your ears, by cutting off all vain curiosity, which is often the cause of the distractions which beset you in your [spiritual] exercises.   II, 678, 679.

16

May faith be the torch which illuminates, animates and sustains you, so that all your actions and sufferings may be for God alone Who should be served in privation as well as in consolation.   II, 714.

17

Do not distress yourself on account of any distaste or dryness you experience in God's service. He wills that you should serve Him fervently and constantly it is true, but without any other help than simple faith, and thus your love will be the more disinterested, and your service the more pleasing to Him. II, 669.

18

You must take no notice of these thoughts of vanity, but say to Satan, when he suggests them to you in any of your actions: Begone, Satan, I not only renounce thee, but also thy evil suggestions. I did not begin for thee, and I will not end for thee. II, 683.

19

If you find yourself overwhelmed by distractions, collect your thoughts in the tranquil depths of the Sacred Heart. Our Lord will infallibly give you the victory over these distractions provided you fight vigorously against them. II, 754.

20

Do not cling to spiritual consolation, for it is not lasting; on the contrary, seek God by faith, and remember that He has a right to our love no less when He tries us than when He consoles us. II, 683.

21

When through dryness or distraction of mind, you feel unable to form any good thought at mental prayer, offer to the Eternal Father the prayer the Sacred Heart makes for you in the Blessed Sacrament, thus to supply for your insufficiency.

II, 721.

22

We must not belong to God by halves; as God gives Himself entirely to the soul He loves, so does He desire to possess the soul's entire love.

II, 506.

23

Since God Himself is all greatness, He takes pleasure in lowering His greatness to our littleness, that He may be glorified in our infirmity.

II, 248.

24

Jesus Christ is the true Friend of our hearts, for they are made for Him alone; therefore they can find neither rest, joy nor fullness of content save in Him—so let us love Him with all our strength.

II, 259.

25

One thing the adorable Heart of Jesus asks of Its friends, viz: purity of intention, humility in action and singleness of purpose.   II, 481.

26

Never forget Him Who died for love of you. You will only love Him in so far as you know how to suffer in silence, preferring Him to creatures and eternity to time. II, 646.

27

My only desire would be to remain in silence, or else to speak only of God, for in this my heart takes so great a delight that it can never tire of so doing. II, 137.

28

The Sacred Heart of Jesus is a burning furnace in which our hearts, so cowardly and cold, so faulty and imperfect, are tried and purified as gold in the crucible, in order that they be offered to Him as living victims, wholly immolated and sacrificed to His adorable designs. II, 411.

29

Our Lord frequently told me that I should keep a secluded place for Him in my heart ... where He would teach me to love Him. II, 132.

30

O my Jesus and my Love, take all that I have and all that I am and possess me to the full extent of Thy good pleasure, since all I have is Thine without reserve. Transform me entirely into Thyself, so that I may no longer be able to separate myself from Thee for a single moment, and

that I may no longer act but by the impulse of
Thy pure love.   II, 137.

31
On coming away from prayer I used to say: "O
my Jesus, as I cannot remain in Thy presence, I
would rather die than be separated from Thee by
sin. Come Thou with me to sanctify all my actions, since all are done for Thee."   II, 148.

JUNE

The Holy Eucharist—The Sacred Heart

1

Let every knee bend before Thee, O greatness of my God, so supremely humbled in the Sacred Host. May every heart love Thee, every spirit adore Thee and every will be subject to Thee!

II, 197.

2

Jesus makes Himself poor in the Blessed Sacrament; He gives us all He has, reserving nothing for Himself, so as to possess our hearts and enrich them with Himself. I must forsake and despise myself, if I wish to imitate Him and to win His most lovable Heart.

II, 741.

3

As I was about to receive Holy Communion, our Lord told me that He would come Himself to imprint on my heart the mystical life which He leads in the holy Eucharist, a life entirely hidden and annihilated in the eyes of men, a life of sacrifice and seeming inactivity. He added that He would Himself give me the strength to do what He required of me.

II, 198.

4

Jesus was obedient even to the death of the Cross, therefore I wish to obey even to my last sigh, so as to pay homage to the obedience of Jesus in the Sacred Host; and the whiteness of the Host teaches me that I must be a pure victim, in order to be sacrificed to Him.   II, 197.

5

I will unite all my prayers with those that the Sacred Heart of Jesus makes for us in the Blessed Sacrament.   II, 197.

6

My greatest happiness is to be before the Blessed Sacrament, where my heart is, as it were, in Its center.   II, 137.

7

What increases my sufferings is that I cannot avenge upon myself the insults that are offered to my divine Saviour in the most holy Sacrament of the Altar.   II, 394.

8

God is so good that He allows us to appropriate this treasure of the really poor—the Sacred Heart of Jesus—the heavenly plenitude of Which can most fully supply for what is lacking to us. II, 232.

9

The Sacred Heart is a hidden and infinite treasure desiring to manifest Itself, to be poured out and distributed, so as to alleviate our distress.

II, 405.

10

It seems to me that the great desire that our Lord has that His Sacred Heart should be honored by some particular worship is to renew in souls the effects of His Redemption. II, 321.

11

He has given me to understand that His Sacred Heart is the Holy of Holies—the Sanctuary of Love—that He wills to be known at present as the Mediator between God and man; for He is all-powerful to reconcile them, turning aside the chastisements that our sins have merited and obtaining mercy for us. II, 300.

12

Our Lord Jesus Christ desires that we should, by sanctifying ourselves, glorify His all-loving Heart; for it was His Heart that suffered the most in His Sacred Humanity. II, 556.

13

This divine Heart experienced all the interior sufferings of the cruel torment of the Cross, and for this reason God wishes It to be honored by a special worship, in order that mankind may thereby atone by their love and homage, for the

bitterness and anguish caused by their offences.
II, 556.

14

I no longer wish for anything but to procure the
glory of the Sacred Heart. How happy I should be
if, before I die, I were able to do something to
please Him!   II, 302.

15

I feel entirely lost in this divine Heart. It is as
though I were in a fathomless abyss, in which He
discloses to me treasures of love and of grace for
those who consecrate and sacrifice themselves to
give and procure for Him all the honor, love and
glory in their power.   II, 396.

16

I can hardly express my joy at seeing the increase of devotion to the Sacred Heart of my
Saviour. I seem to live for that alone. Sometimes
such an ardent desire to make It reign in all hearts
is kindled within me that there is nothing I would
not do and suffer to bring this about.   II, 304.

17

He has assured me that the pleasure He takes
in being loved, known and honored by His
creatures, is so great that, if I am not mistaken,
He has promised me that all those who are
devoted and consecrated to Him shall never
perish.   II, 300.

18

The devotion to His Sacred Heart contains ineffable treasures which He wishes to bestow upon all hearts of goodwill; it is a last effort of the love of our Lord towards sinners to draw them to repentance and give them in abundance His efficacious and sanctifying graces.   II, 445.

19

He is the Source of all blessings, and will bestow them wherever the picture of His divine Heart is placed and honored.   II, 300.

20

I believe that He will confirm these words which His unworthy slave continually heard in the depths of her heart, amidst all the difficulties and opposition that beset the beginning of this devotion: "I shall reign in spite of My enemies and of all those who would oppose Me." II, 537.

21

Would that I could exhaust myself in acts of thanksgiving and gratitude towards this divine Heart, for the great favor He shows us, in deigning to accept our help to make Him known, loved and honored; He reserves infinite blessings for all those who devote themselves to this work.

II, 531.

22

Were it but possible for me to reveal the infinite riches that are hidden in this precious treasure, with which He enriches and benefits His faithful friends! Could we but understand, we should spare no pains to procure Him the satisfaction He so ardently desires.   II, 533.

23

He has so fashioned and destined me for His all-lovable Heart, that He alone is all my joy, my consolation, my treasure and my happiness; and apart from Him all else is as nothing to me.

II, 556.

24

My sole interest henceforth is the Sacred Heart of my Saviour, and I would die happy if I had procured It some honor, even at the cost of eternal suffering as a reward. Provided that I love Him and that He reigns, I am content.   II, 301.

25

My divine Master has taught me to look upon myself only as the sport of the good pleasure of His adorable Heart, my sole treasure, and in this it is that I must glory.   II, 253.

26

I seem to be as a little drop of water in the ocean of the Sacred Heart, Which is a deep of every kind of blessing, an inexhaustible fount of delight; the more one draws from this source, the more abundantly It flows.   II, 404.

27

There is nothing sweeter and milder, and at the same time stronger and more efficacious than the gentle unction of the burning charity of this lovable Heart, to convert the most hardened souls and to penetrate the most unfeeling hearts.   II, 557.

28

If you would live entirely for Him, and reach the perfection which He desires of you, you must sacrifice yourself unreservedly with all that depends on you. You must no longer will anything but by the will of this loving Heart, and no longer love anything but by Its affections. You must act only by Its light; never undertake anything without first asking for Its counsel and help; give It all the glory thereof; return It thanks, both for failure and for success in your undertakings, and without worrying be equally satisfied with all; for, provided that this divine Heart is pleased, loved and glorified, nothing else matters.   II, 281.

29

Let us not be grieved if our desires for the glory of the divine Heart are not at once fulfilled. This delay is only permitted because He takes pleasure in seeing the increase of our zeal and eagerness for His glory.   II, 480.

30

This Feast [of the Sacred Heart] is a day of salvation and of eternal blessing for all who honor It with a humble and sincere heart. Let us, then, love this divine Heart and in all things try to conform ourselves to It. II, 444.

JULY

Love of God

1

On awaking, enter in the Sacred Heart of Jesus and consecrate to It your body, your soul, your heart and your whole being, so as to live but for Its love and glory alone.   II, 718.

2

Our heart is too small to contain two loves, being made only for divine love, it finds no rest in any other.   II, 423.

3

Divine love suffices to prevent us from willfully doing anything which could displease the Beloved of our souls. Indeed, I cannot understand how a heart that belongs to God and truly wishes to love Him, can deliberately offend Him.
II, 375.

4

I see more clearly than the day that a life without the love of Jesus Christ is the greatest of all miseries.   I, 268.

5

Let us apply ourselves only to love and to suffer while loving. When we have acquired the perfect knowledge thereof, then we shall know and do all that God wishes of us.　　II, 239.

6

Never forget Him Who died for love of you. You will only love Him in so far as you know how to suffer in silence, preferring Him to creatures and eternity to time.　　II, 646.

7

If we wish to have the love of the divine Heart as our guest, we must empty and detach our heart from its affection for creatures and for ourselves.
　　II, 725.

8

As it is love alone which produces in us the desire of conformity with our Sovereign Master, we can only attain to this conformity by loving Him supremely.　　II, 248.

9

You ask me for some short prayer by which to testify your love for God. I know of and consider nothing more efficacious than this same love, for when one loves, everything speaks of love, even our most absorbing occupations can be a proof of our love. Love then—as St. Augustine says—and do what you will.　　II, 420.

10

I love my Sovereign Master and think more of Him than of His gifts and benefits, which I esteem only in Him and as coming from Him.

II, 401.

11

My heart can neither love nor be attached to aught but to Him alone. All else is nothing and serves but to hinder the purity of love, and to raise a barrier between the soul and her Beloved.

II, 253.

12

Grant, O my God, that throughout my life, I may love Thee with true, ardent and persevering love.

II, 795.

13

Why do we not burn with the divine fire which He has come to enkindle on earth! We ought to be consumed therein. To love and be consumed by this sacred fire will be my constant endeavor.

II, 480.

14

Assuredly there is no one in the world who would not receive every kind of help from Heaven, if he had a truly grateful love for Jesus Christ, such as that which is shown by devotion to His Sacred Heart.

II, 623.

15

If we love this sovereign Good and forget ourselves, all will be well.   II, 454.

16

Let us love Him, then, this only Love of our
souls, since He has first loved us and still loves us
with burning ardor in the Blessed Sacrament. We
have only to love this All-Holy One, to become
holy: who can prevent us from being so, since we
have a heart to love and a body to suffer? II, 473.

17

Either die or conquer.... There must be no
reserve in love.   II, 54, 60.

18

In order to make good use of time we must
love ardently and constantly; we must surrender
ourselves entirely to love, leaving it to act for us.
Be satisfied to adhere to it in everything, but always with profound humility.   II, 748.

19

Do everything through love and for love, making good use of the present moment, and do not
be anxious about the future.   II, 709.

20

Taking your heart, as it were, in your hands,
offer and consecrate it to our Lord, that He may
be forever the sole Owner thereof, that He may

reign therein absolutely and may teach you to love Him perfectly.   II, 661.

21

It is attachment to creatures and to self-satisfaction that weakens the blessing of love in your heart. You must die to all that, if you wish the pure love of God to reign therein.   II, 670.

22

Our Lord loves you and wishes to see you advance with great speed in the way of His love, however crucifying to nature. Therefore, do not bargain with Him, but give Him all, and you will find all in His divine Heart.   II, 375.

23

We must love this Sacred Heart, with all our strength and with all our capacity. Yes, we must love Him, and He will establish His empire and will reign in spite of all His enemies and their opposition.   II, 401.

24

Let us ask Him to strengthen our weakness, to enrich our poverty, to soften the hardness of our hearts so as to make them susceptible to His pure love, which will not be content with a divided heart.   II, 725.

25

Our heart is made for God. Woe, then, if it be

satisfied with less than God, or if it allow itself to
burn with any other fire than that of His pure
love!   II, 168.

26

Since, in His mercy, He has consecrated me to
His love and to His glory, I care not in what manner He treats me. Provided He is satisfied, I am
content. Whether He raises me up or casts me
down, consoles or afflicts me, it is all the same to
me, as long as His good pleasure is fulfilled.

II, 533.

27

The love of creatures is as poison in your heart
and destroys the love of Jesus Christ. If you seek
the esteem of creatures and try to insinuate yourself into their good graces, you will lose those of
the Sacred Heart. You will be deprived of Its
treasures in proportion as you enrich yourself
with created things.   II, 711.

28

Your love for God must be so great that grace
may triumph over your heart and over all human
respect. No more self-introspection. Provided
that the good pleasure of the Sacred Heart is accomplished, suffering or enjoyment must be a
matter of indifference to you.   II, 700.

29

Love Him with all your strength, think always

of Him, let Him do with you, in you and for you, whatever He wills, and do not be anxious about anything else.   II, 665.

30

Take for your motto: Love has conquered me, it alone shall possess my heart.   II, 693.

31

Love means suffering. He has shown us this plainly upon the Cross where He sacrificed Himself for love of us, and He continues to do so daily in the Blessed Sacrament of the Altar. He ardently desires that we should conform our life to His, which is wholly hidden and annihilated in the eyes of creatures.   II, 336.

AUGUST

Love of One's Neighbor
Charity—Humility

1

While at prayer, I begged our Lord to make known to me by what means I could satisfy the desire that I had to love Him. He gave me to understand, that one cannot better show one's love for Him than by loving one's neighbor for love of Him; and that I must work for the salvation of others, forgetting my own interests in order to espouse those of my neighbor, both in my prayers and in all the good I might be able to do by the mercy of God.   II, 128.

2

Bear patiently the little vexations caused by your neighbor's being of a disposition contrary to your own; do not show your resentment, for that displeases the Sacred Heart of our Lord. II, 692.

3

Our Lord wishes us to have great charity for our neighbor, for whom we should pray as for ourselves; it is one of the characteristic effects of this devotion to reconcile hearts and to bring peace to souls.   II, 557.

4

Work courageously and untiringly in the vineyard of the Lord, for this is the price of your crown; you must forget yourself and all your own interests and think only of increasing His glory in the work He has confided to you.   II, 484.

5

You see plainly that I do not mean to advise you to perform great austerities, but rather generously to mortify your passions and inclinations, detaching your heart and emptying it of all that is earthly, and exercising charity towards your neighbor and liberality towards the poor.

II, 389.

6

You should never find fault with, accuse or judge anyone but yourself, so that your lips that are destined to praise God, and your tongue on which the Sacred Host so often rests, may not serve Satan as instruments to sully your soul.

II, 683.

7

Never keep up any coldness towards your neighbor, or else the Sacred Heart of Jesus Christ will keep aloof from you. When you resentfully call to mind former slights that you have received, you oblige our Lord to recall your past sins which His mercy had made Him forget.

II, 720.

8

Be meek and gentle, affable and charitable towards your neighbor; but do not give him what you owe to the Sacred Heart of our Lord. II, 678.

9

Plunge yourself often into the charity of that lovable Heart so that you may never act towards your neighbor in a manner which may, in the least, wound that virtue, never doing to others what you would not wish done to yourself.

II, 755.

10

The virtue of meekness will make you condescending towards your neighbor whom you will excuse, bearing charitably and in silence all the pain which may be caused you.   II, 744.

11

You will not dispute nor show your repugnance and aversion, for meekness makes us bear everything without complaining.   II, 744.

12

Above all, let us carefully keep silence on occasions that mortify us. Let us be charitable and humble, both in our thoughts and words. II, 319.

13

If you wish to become a disciple of the Sacred Heart of Jesus, you must conform yourself to His

divine maxims and be meek and humble like
Him.   II, 715.

14

He will have a special love and care for you, if
you keep yourself interiorly humble, and strive to
be gentle and steadfast in suffering abjection in
humiliations, which are often the harder to bear
the more trifling they are.   II, 675.

15

Be humble towards God and gentle with your
neighbor. Judge and accuse no one but yourself,
and ever excuse others. Speak of God always to
praise and glorify Him, speak of your neighbor
only with respect—do not speak of yourself at all,
either well or ill.   II, 708.

16

Avoid over-eagerness and strive to model your
interior and exterior upon the humble sweetness
of the loving Heart of Jesus, doing each of your
actions with the same tranquillity as if you had
but that alone to do.   II, 696.

17

He wishes you to conform your heart to the
virtues of His own. If you only knew how much
you grieve Him when you fail in charity or
humility, or when, through cowardice, you
neglect to use the lights He gives you to make you

withdraw from dissipation and self-introspection!
                                        II, 706.

18

Consider often that it is only the humble of
heart that can enter into the Sacred Heart of Jesus
Christ, converse with Him, love Him and be
loved by Him.   II, 746.

19

Conform yourself as closely as possible to His
humility and gentleness in dealing with your
neighbor ... Love those who humble and con-
tradict you, for they are more useful to your perfection than those who flatter you.   II, 673.

20

Be humble and courageous in not giving way to
despondency on account of your faults or of the
slight vexations and humiliations with which you
may meet.   II, 677.

21

We must endeavor to the utmost of our power
to enter into the adorable Heart of our Lord by
making ourselves very little and humbly confess-
ing our nothingness, thus losing sight of self entirely.   II, 418.

22

I will do my utmost to be gentle and sub-

missive, stifling any feelings of resentment or
repugnance.   II, 661.

23

Humble yourself whenever opportunity offers
with true humility of heart. This is all, I think,
that the Heart of our Lord asks of you.   II, 716.

24

You must offer yourself to God as a mere
nothing to its Creator Who, finding no resistance,
will give it such being as pleases Him.   II, 710.

25

Keep yourself lowly and little in your own
eyes, that thus you may grow in this divine Heart.
                                         II, 714.

26

I think that, according to what our Lord makes
known to me, He does not wish to take away
from you these feelings contrary to the virtue of
humility; He leaves you something to fight
against, so that He may reward your victories;
and also, that you may be continually on your
guard and have a great distrust of yourself. II, 540.

27

You must be very careful to profit by the occasions of mortification and humiliation that come
in your way, not avoiding or shunning them, for

they are the principal means of uniting yourself
to the Sacred Heart of Jesus.   II, 701.

28

I have indeed thanked the Sacred Heart of our
Lord Jesus Christ for the graces that He gives
you, and I have besought Him to continue to
bestow them upon you and to make you correspond faithfully with them, so that you may persevere steadfastly in the holy desires He gives
you to love and glorify Him by making Him
known.   II, 357.

29

Above all, He wishes you to be humble of heart
like Him and always full of charity. You will practice these two virtues according to the light this
divine Heart will give you.   II, 761.

30

This divine Heart is naught but sweetness,
humility and patience, therefore, we must
wait . . . He knows when to act.   II, 449.

31

If you find yourself in an abyss of pride and of
vain self-esteem, plunge yourself at once into the
abyss of the humility of the Sacred Heart. There
you must submerge all feelings of pride that are
stirred up within you, so that by love of your own
abjection you may clothe yourself with His sacred
annihilations.   II, 753.

SEPTEMBER

Self-effacement—Detachment

1

Behold, O my soul, the means by which you can honor your God, viz., by renouncing and humbling yourself with Jesus Christ and for the love of Jesus Christ. Thus you will find life in death, sweetness in bitterness, and God in self-effacement: for you must leave all in order to find Him. II, 168.

2

As all things find rest only in their center and are irresistibly drawn to what is natural to them, even so my heart, wholly absorbed in its center, the humble Heart of Jesus, has an unquenchable thirst for humiliations, contempt and oblivion on the part of creatures, and thus I never feel happier than when I am conformed to my crucified Spouse. II, 179.

3

I must efface and annihilate myself and live poor, unknown, forgotten and despised by creatures and hidden in the Sacred Heart of my divine Master, so that He may found His Kingdom on my nothingness. II, 497.

4

O my God, Thou mayest indeed destroy and annihilate me, but I will not leave Thee till Thou hast granted me the conversion of these hearts.

II, 155.

5

This Sovereign of our souls takes delight only in a truly humble soul; and in order to live wholly to Him we must no longer live to ourselves.

II, 386.

6

I assure you I possess naught but my Saviour Jesus Christ. Therefore He often says to me: "What wouldst thou do without Me? Thou wouldst be poor indeed!" II, 253.

7

I wish to learn in the Sacred Heart of Jesus to suffer all things in silence, and never to complain of what may be done to me, since dust deserves but to be trodden underfoot. II, 191.

8

Be despoiled of everything and the Sacred Heart of Jesus will enrich you. Empty your heart of everything and He will compensate you. Forget and abandon yourself. II, 695.

9

He will raise you to union with Himself in proportion as He finds you lowered in your own estimation. Do everything, therefore, through love and from a motive of humility.   II, 710.

10

Know that if you wish to possess Jesus Christ and to dwell in His Sacred Heart, you must have no other desire and be content with Him alone.
II, 749.

11

I can say nothing more, except that the effacement of yourself will raise you to union with your Sovereign Good. By forgetting self, you will possess Him, and by yielding yourself up to Him, He will possess you.   II, 432.

12

May He teach you what He desires of you, and may He give you the strength to accomplish it perfectly! If I am not mistaken this, in a few words, is what I think He chiefly requires of you: He wishes that you should learn to live without support—without a friend—and without satisfaction. In proportion as you ponder over these words, He will help you to understand them.
II, 411.

13

We must be content with and conformed to His most holy Will, stripped and destitute of pleasure,

friends, consolation, talents, and aware of our
lack of virtue.   II, 423.

14

Our Lord would fain be your sole Support,
Friend and Delight, provided you seek neither
support nor delight in creatures. Nevertheless,
you must not be ill at ease or constrained in your
intercourse with your neighbor, but always humble, bright, kind and gracious in your manner.

II, 666.

15

Frankly, I do not think the favors which our
Lord promises you, to consist in an abundance of
temporal things: for He says that these often
deprive us of His grace and of His love, whereas it
is with these latter gifts that He wishes to enrich
your soul.   II, 481.

16

No longer heed the feelings of immortified
nature, nor the suggestions of self-love, which
clamors to have, to possess, to keep and to hoard
up. Let it cry out as much as it likes; we belong to
the Sacred Heart of Jesus Christ, and we must
have only what He wishes us to have, and be glad
to be like Him, stripped of all things.   II, 749.

17

Do not cling or cleave to earthly things; keep
your heart aloof from them as much as you can.

Let there be no human respect where the glory of
God is concerned.   II, 366.

18

Love the Sacred Heart ardently and It will help
you to overcome yourself, to humble yourself,
and to detach yourself from creatures and from
self.   II, 704.

19

As for the ardent desire which urges you to
become a saint, I hope this will be so, with the
grace of the Sacred Heart of our Lord Who will
make you a great saint, but I think He will
sanctify you in His own way and not in yours.
Therefore you must leave it to Him, and have no
other end in view than to glorify Him by self-
effacement; He in His turn will look upon you to
purify and sanctify you. (To Rev. Father
Croiset).   II, 602.

20

The Sacred Heart of Jesus Christ gives you
these holy aspirations through the ardent love He
bears you, which makes Him desire to possess
your heart whole and entire.   II, 443.

21

The soul that is the humblest and most
despised will be most loved by His adorable
Heart. The most despoiled and stripped of all
things will possess It more fully.   II, 730.

22

You must offer yourself to God as a mere nothing to its Creator Who, finding no resistance, will give it such being as pleases Him.   II, 710.

23

Love to be looked upon as a mere nothing in the house of God.   II, 709.

24

Cherish and honor those who humble and mortify you; look upon them as your greatest benefactors, and say to yourself: Were I known for what I really am, it would be evident that I deserve far more humiliations.   II, 709.

25

Look upon that lowly path as the real one our Lord has traced out for us, and the surest to reach Him. Walk steadily therein in peace and thanksgiving.   II, 386.

26

If you are in the depths of poverty, stripped of all and of self, go and lose yourself in the Sacred Heart of Jesus. He will enrich you and will take delight in clothing you [with His own perfections] if you allow Him to act.   II, 753.

27

Now I shall die happy, since the Sacred Heart of my Saviour is beginning to be known; for it seems to me that, through His mercy, I am almost wholly stripped and divested of esteem and reputation in the minds of others, which consoles me more than I can say.   II, 322.

28

Our Lord continues to give me many graces, unworthy though I be; that which I prize the most is conformity to His life of suffering and humiliation. He keeps me in such a state of entire submission to His good pleasure, that I am indifferent to all else.   II, 288.

29

Let us beg this lovable Heart to establish this devotion firmly and to fill with the unction of Its grace and of Its ardent charity all whom It will send us. I would willingly die that He might reign!   II, 390.

30

The reason why I am not permitted to speak of the rewards which He promises to those whom He will employ in this holy work, is that they may act without any other motive than that of His glory and for love of Him alone.   II, 551.

OCTOBER

Love of the Cross, Contempt and Suffering

1

What shall I render to the Lord for the great blessings He has bestowed upon me? O my God, how great is Thy goodness towards me in thus permitting me to sit at the table of the Saints, and partake of the same viands with which Thou didst sustain them. Thou dost give me to eat abundantly and provide me, an unworthy and miserable sinner, with the refection given to Thy intimate and most faithful friends. Truly, without the Blessed Sacrament and the cross, I could not live, nor could I bear my long exile.   II, 97.

2

Life without the cross would be unbearable. All happiness here below consists in being able to suffer.   II, 184.

3

Crosses, contempt, sorrows and afflictions are the real treasures of the lovers of Jesus Christ crucified.   II, 244.

4

Prostrating myself at the foot of my Crucifix I

said: "How happy should I be, O my loving Savior, if Thou wouldst imprint on me the likeness of Thy sufferings." To which He replied: "This is what I intend to do, provided thou dost not resist Me and on thy side dost contribute thereto."   II, 50.

5

In God's sight, our cross is as a precious balm which loses its aroma on exposure to the air; therefore we must make every effort to hide our cross and carry it in silence.   II, 422.

6

I think He intends to try you like gold in the crucible, so as to number you amongst His most faithful servants. Therefore you must lovingly embrace all occasions of suffering, considering them as precious tokens of His love. To suffer in silence and without complaint is what He asks of you.   II, 699.

7

No other grace can be compared with that of carrying the cross out of love for our Lord.
                                                II, 247.

8

The cross is a precious treasure to be kept secret, lest we be robbed of it.   II, 412.

9

My words would have been useless, had they not touched upon the Cross of our divine Lord. You are indeed blest, if you know how to carry, embrace and cherish it, for love of Him Who, for love of us, has loved it so much.   II, 238.

10

I was greatly consoled by the pleasure you gave our Lord in embracing His cross with joy and submission. It is true that He covered it entirely with roses, lest it should frighten you. But it is not so much in this that you should rejoice, but rather that you feel the pricks of the thorns hidden beneath.   II, 231.

11

What should I do, had I not a cross to bear? . . . It is my whole treasure in the adorable Heart of Jesus Christ, and there it is the cause of all my happiness, my delight and my joy.   II, 240.

12

This is the thought He wishes me to dwell upon:
    "The cross do I glory to bear,
    And love to it leadeth me e'er;
    Love divine my entire being doth own,
    And for me, love sufficeth alone."   II, 289.

13

Nothing unites us so closely to the Sacred

Heart of our Lord Jesus Christ as the cross which is the most precious pledge of His love.   II, 422.

14

You must constantly carry the cross which He lays on you, be it interior or exterior, without growing weary or complaining of its length or weight. Does it not suffice that it has been given you by the hands of a Friend Whose all-loving Heart had destined it for you from all eternity?

II, 712.

15

Trust to the goodness of our Lord in the crosses which He sends you; He will never abandon you, for He knows how to draw good from our ills and His glory from our trials.   II, 505.

16

Thanks be to God, I am poor in every respect, and I desire to be rich only in the pure love of His sufferings and humiliations: Jesus, His love and His cross constitute all the happiness of life.

II, 329.

17

I seem not to have suffered anything as yet and, consequently, I feel I have done nothing for my God.   II, 247.

18

I know of no other happiness in life than to re-

main ever hidden in our nothingness—to suffer
and love in silence—to embrace our crosses,
praising and thanking Him Who gives them to us.
                                                    II, 258.

19

Suffer bravely, and be content that the divine
good pleasure be accomplished in you. You must
ever be immolated and sacrificed to it with
unshaken trust that the Sacred Heart will not forsake you: It is closer to you in suffering than in
consolation.   II, 700.

20

Take up your abode in the lovable Heart of
Jesus, and you will find therein imperturbable
peace and the strength to carry out the good
desires He gives you. Bring to this divine Heart all
your troubles and afflictions, for whatever ema-
nates from the Sacred Heart is sweet: It changes
everything into love.   II, 235.

21

Our Lord will delight in making you conformable to Him, and will show you that He is not less
worthy of being loved when your soul is filled
with the bitterness of Calvary, than when it is en-
joying the delights of Thabor.   II, 231.

22

He would make you merit the crown He has
destined for you, by giving you some small share

in the sufferings He endured during the whole of His mortal life, and you are indeed happy, whatever trials you may be enduring, to be thus in conformity with Him.   II, 642.

23

The bitterest sorrow is but sweetness in this adorable Heart, where everything is changed into love.   II, 393.

24

When you have anything to suffer, rejoice and unite it to that which the Sacred Heart has suffered and still suffers in the Blessed Sacrament.   II, 720.

25

When my sufferings increase, I feel the same joy that the most miserly and ambitious experience as they see their treasures increase.

II, 295.

26

I am so happy to have no other tokens of affection or consolation from creatures than crosses and humiliations, and never had I more of them. I write these few lines to you by the way, to invite you to give thanks to the Sacred Heart for me.

II, 368.

27

I feel such great sorrow at having offended

Thee, O infinite Goodness, that I fain would suffer all the punishment due not only to the sins I have committed, but also to those into which I should have fallen, had it not been for the help of Thy grace.   II, 206.

28

The cross is good at all times and in all places. It matters little of what wood it is made, provided that it is offered to us by the Sacred Heart of our Lord.   II, 392.

29

To wish to love God without suffering for love of Him is but illusion. Still, I cannot understand that one can suffer, if one really loves the Sacred Heart of our Lord Jesus Christ, because He changes the bitterest gall into sweetness. II, 467.

30

Let us love the Sacred Heart upon the Cross, since It delights to find in a heart love, silence and suffering.   II, 466.

31

There can be no consolation for me but to see the reign of the Heart of my adorable Saviour. Whenever this devotion makes some progress, He always favors me with some unusual suffering.   II, 393.

NOVEMBER

Various Subjects

1

I hope all from the Sacred Heart of our Lord
Jesus Christ Who is so filled with love for you
that, cost what it may, He wills you should
become a saint. (To her brother, the priest.)

II, 344.

2

In a word, let us be all to God, all for God and
all in God; and remember that He wills you to
lead an exemplary life, wholly pure and angelic.
(To the same.) II, 345.

3

Do not think that to work for the salvation of
the souls He has entrusted to you is an obstacle to
your own salvation. On the contrary, by this
means you will oblige His Goodness to give you
greater help to work it out with less danger.
Watch carefully, therefore, over your little flock.
(To the same.) II, 366.

4

I am very glad that our divine Master has

shown you that these trials add to the burden of
your office; for He wishes them to be the cause of
your having more frequent recourse to His Goodness, which will turn all these things to His glory
and to your advantage, if you second His designs.
(To a Superioress.)   II, 255.

5

May the Sacred Heart accomplish in you all His
designs and be Himself your strength and your
stay, so as to enable you to bear courageously the
weight of your responsibility.   II, 257.

6

As you are of good will, I am sure that if you
are faithful, the Sacred Heart will help you to
make this sacrifice which will draw upon you
many blessings. But you must not think this can
be done all at once and without a struggle; there
must be many a battle. To gain the victory you
must persevere.   II, 702.

7

What regret would be yours at the hour of
death, should you see yourself deprived of the
crown which awaits you if you are faithful in
generously following the light that our Lord gives
you. And, to tell the truth, you will only find
peace and rest when you have sacrificed all for
God.   II, 351.

8

Strive ever to have a loving and filial fear, which will lead you to do good and avoid evil, rejecting all other fears, for they only come from the spirit of darkness. II, 669.

9

Let us take refuge in the Wound of the Sacred Side like a poor traveller, who seeks a safe harbor in which to shelter from the rocks and tempests of the stormy sea of this life, for here below we are continually exposed to shipwreck, unless we have the help of our all-wise Pilot. II, 724.

10

Provided He is pleased we ought to be satisfied, and ought not to be troubled about our feelings of dissatisfaction or annoyance; these arise within us only because we are not sufficiently mortified and simple-hearted to cut off the windings and reflections of self-love. II, 274.

11

Above all, I beg of you to be always gay, joyful and happy, for this is the true mark of the Spirit of God, Who wishes that we should serve Him in peace and contentment; do not be uneasy or anxious, but do all things with liberty of mind and in the presence of God. II, 232.

12

If He so wills, God can draw His glory from our most insignificant actions.   II, 232.

13

When you fail in simplicity and humility, you lose the friendship of the Sacred Heart. Your heart is then left like barren soil which only produces the thorns and thistles of faults and imperfections—this refers to willful faults.   II, 658.

14

I do not know why God inspires me to speak so often of simplicity, unless it be that He seems to me to have such horror of the contrary. Were I to see in a soul all the other virtues without that of simplicity, were it even favored with all those graces which our Lord bestows on His dearest friends—all would seem to be but deceit and illusion.   II, 276.

15

He loves you and would not have you attach yourself to what is perishable, but to Himself Who alone can satisfy your heart, and He will do so and fill it in the measure in which you empty it of creatures.   II, 648.

16

When you praise yourself, you become an object of horror and contempt before God and His angels. When you wish to make excuses, say to yourself: "Jesus Who was innocent kept silence when He was accused, and shall I who am guilty justify myself?" Keep silence then, and suffer out of love.   II, 652.

17

In all your needs, trustfully have recourse to the divine Heart, and I am confident that our Lord will provide for your wants; but above all be very grateful for the many benefits He has bestowed on you.   II, 665.

18

I cannot but admire the goodness and liberality of the Sacred Heart towards you. Our Lord seems to take pleasure in unfolding all Its treasures for your benefit.   II, 759.

19

Your name will be written in this Sacred Heart in indelible characters.   II, 306.

20

The things that immediately concern the glory of God are very different from those of the world, for which much activity is necessary; as regards the things of God, we must be content to follow His inspirations and leave grace to act, co-operating wholeheartedly with its movements.

II, 479.

21

Having once made an entire donation of ourselves, let us not retract it: our Lord will employ every means to sanctify us, in proportion as we make use of every opportunity to glorify Him.

II, 335.

22

We should always look to God as in ourselves, no matter in what manner we meditate upon Him, so as to accustom ourselves to dwell in His divine presence. For when we behold Him within our souls, all our powers and faculties, and even our senses, are recollected within us. If we look at God apart from ourselves we are easily distracted by exterior objects.   II, 726.

23

Love, glory and praise be forever to the Heart of our adorable Saviour, for It is all love, all loving and all lovable!   II, 431.

24

May you no longer have any liberty except to love Him. May no other light illumine your soul, no other aim absorb your heart than that of His pure love which keeps Him a prisoner in the Blessed Sacrament. You will ask Him, through the merits of this captivity, to set free His poor prisoners in Purgatory.   II, 727.

25

How grateful I should be, if you would help me by your prayers to relieve my "dear suffering friends," for so I call them. There is nothing I would not do or suffer to help them. I assure you they are not ungrateful. II, 295.

26

When I commit any faults, after having punished myself for them by penance, I will offer to the Eternal Father one of the virtues of the divine Heart, in order to repair the outrages of which I have been guilty, and thus little by little pay my debt. II, 198.

27

I am fit only to check the flow of God's mercy, be assured of it! To speak truly, I am only a compound of all misery, powerless for good and most unworthy of God's graces. II, 255.

28

I must own that I have never before so fully realized God's goodness to me, for notwithstanding my great misery He does not forsake me. Therefore my only refuge is His adorable Heart Which is ever my surety and my defence.

II, 310.

29

I am attacked on all sides, yet I will not fear, for I keep myself strongly entrenched in my secure fortress—the Sacred Heart of my divine Master. Like a wise leader He deals out to me just strength sufficient for each occasion.   II, 606.

30

I have no pleasure in this miserable life except in what concerns the interests of the Sacred Heart of Jesus Who often fastens me, stripped of all, to the Cross.   II, 295.

DECEMBER

Various Subjects

1

If we knew what we lose when we do not profit by occasions of suffering, we should be far more careful to make good use of such moments.

II, 318.

2

Gently recall your mind when it wanders. You must be prepared to lose all in order to be lost in God.

II, 714.

3

What sustains my weakness is the thought that our Lord is pleased to glorify His infinite mercy by exercising it on the feeblest of His creatures.

II, 281.

4

I beg the Sacred Heart of our loving Jesus, Who is my only treasure, to reward you out of the abundance of His pure love, for He is the inexhaustible Source from which the more one draws, the more there is to draw.

II, 455.

5

The divine Heart is the treasury of Heaven, from which valuable gold has already been given in manifold ways, to pay our debts and purchase Heaven. II, 556.

6

If you find yourself in the depths of spiritual poverty, cast that poverty into the abyss of the adorable Heart of Jesus Which abounds in every kind of good; in this Sacred Heart you will lose what might be the occasion of death to your soul, to find instead, by true mortification, a source of life. II, 754.

7

In the excess of His love, He willed, through the merits of His death, to win for us a life of eternal happiness, and save us from a death of eternal misery. Let us bless and thank Him for such ardent charity. II, 724.

8

Nothing can be more pleasing to God than the honor paid to His holy Mother. II, 738.

9

Take up your abode in this adorable Heart; bring to It your little vexations and annoyances, and your heart will then be calmed. You will find in this divine Heart the remedy for your ills,

strength in your weakness, and a refuge in all
your needs.   II, 708.

10

Since it is not the divine good pleasure to still
the tempest within you, I beg the Sacred Heart to
be Himself your support, so that you may remain
firm, immovable and tranquil in the midst of the
storm, which must not disturb you at all, for it
cannot overpower you.   II, 676.

11

Have no reserve with Him Who wishes to
dwell within you as the source of eternal life. He
would reign in you, to rule and govern you, by
being the motive power of all your actions and
the object of all your affections.   II, 643.

12

This divine Heart wishes to be the absolute
Master of yours. . . . It is the inexhaustible Source
of all good, and seeks especially to give and communicate Itself to faithful souls.   II, 328.

13

Let us entreat Him to establish His reign in all
hearts. Let us contribute thereto with all our
power; in order to do this, let us spare neither life
nor possessions.   II, 446.

14

I admire the mercy of God with regard to the

dear departed one. .... Happy the soul who has quitted this miserable life where there is nothing but suffering and affliction of mind, and where our salvation is constantly endangered through sin, the greatest enemy of the soul.   II, 484.

15

What are the joys of life where nothing is lasting? They pass like a dream, and I cannot understand how a heart which loves God and which seeks Him can take any pleasure save in Him alone.   II, 258.

16

Endeavor to take all your delight in this divine Heart, and beg the most Holy Trinity to make It known and loved by all hearts that are capable of so doing.   II, 665.

17

You can hardly realize what pleasure you give me by your zeal for the glory of the Sacred Heart. It is, I think, one of the quickest means of sanctifying oneself.   II, 365.

18

I have indeed thanked the Sacred Heart of our Lord Jesus Christ for the graces that He gives you, and I have besought Him to continue to bestow them upon you, and to make you correspond faithfully with them, that you may persevere steadfastly in the holy desires He gives

you to love and glorify Him by making Him
known.   II, 357.

19

I tell you in particular, according as He gives
me to understand, that the treasures of His Sacred
Heart are open to you. I see He intends to make
you draw abundantly therefrom, and will even
bestow them upon you with profusion.   II, 559.

20

The adorable Heart of Jesus wills to establish
Its reign of love in every heart, so as to overthrow
that of Satan. It seems to me that He so greatly
desires this that He promises great rewards to
those who, with good will and in good earnest,
devote themselves to it, according to the means
and to the light He grants them.   II, 489.

21

I think our Lord is like a king who does not
give rewards whilst he is engaged in fighting bat-
tles and overcoming his enemies, but when he
reigns victorious on his throne.   II, 489.

22

In spite of all opposition, this divine Heart will
eventually triumph. Satan with all his adherents
will be confounded. Happy will they be who have
been the means of establishing His empire.
                                         II, 489.

23

He will reign in spite of His enemies, and will make Himself master of the hearts which He desires to possess; for the principal end of devotion to the Sacred Heart of Jesus is to convert souls to His love.   II, 355.

24

As often as you can, make the following aspiration: I adore Thee and love Thee, O divine Heart of Jesus, living in the heart of Mary; I beseech Thee to live and reign in all hearts and to perfect them in Thy pure love.   II, 751.

25

In order to abide forever in this divine Heart, we must love It with a love of preference, as the one object necessary to our heart, and this love must gradually lead us to despise and forget all else.   II, 418.

26

Since this divine Heart is mine, what can be wanting to me? And if I am entirely His, who can harm me?   II, 763.

27

Devotion to the Sacred Heart of Jesus must not be constrained; our Lord wishes His love to insinuate itself into our hearts sweetly and gently, penetrating gradually like oil, spreading by degrees like the perfume of precious balm. II, 479.

28

The Sacred Heart is an inexhaustible ocean of blessings in which we must lose all, so as no longer to relish earthly things.   II, 430.

29

How good it is to please the divine Heart of our Lord Who will reward our labors by eternal and ineffable delights!   II, 383.

30

As to those who devote. themselves to making Him known and loved, if I could and were permitted to express what He has revealed to me of the rewards they will receive from this adorable Heart, you would then say with me: "Happy are they whom He will employ in the execution of His designs!"   II, 550.

31

Thou knowest well that I am insolvent. Imprison me, I am willing, provided the prison be that of Thy Sacred Heart. Keep me there a close captive, bound by the chains of Thy love, until I have paid all that I owe Thee . . . and, as I shall never be able to do so, let me be ever a close prisoner.   II, 206.

All from God and nothing from myself!
All to God and nothing to myself!
All for God and nothing for myself!

                II, 191.

THIRTY-THREE VISITS
TO OUR LORD ON THE CROSS

To be made on Fridays.

Having read these pages, some souls may, perhaps, feel the desire of loving the Heart of Jesus more ardently, by living more in accordance with His life, and by praying for the conversion of sinners, this latter being one of the principal ends of the devotion to the Sacred Heart.

There may also be souls who will be glad to know of an apostolate, hidden but real, taught by our Saviour Himself to St. Margaret Mary, with a view to the conversion of sinners, viz., Thirty-three Visits to our Lord on the Cross to be made on Fridays.

This is what the Saint wrote about it: One Friday, during holy Mass, I felt a great desire to honor the sufferings of my crucified Spouse. He told me lovingly that He desired me, every Friday, to adore Him thirty-three times upon the Cross, the throne of His mercy. I was to prostrate myself humbly at His feet, and try to remain there in the dispositions of the Blessed Virgin during His Passion. I was to offer these acts of adoration to the Eternal Father together with the sufferings of her divine Son, to beg of Him the conversion of all hardened and faithless hearts who resist the impulse of His grace. He told me, moreover, that at the hour of death He will be favorable to those who have been faithful to this practice.

These thirty-three acts of adoration of our Lord on the Cross may be made anywhere on Fridays, and even while attending to one's ordinary work. They require no special attitude, formula or vocal prayer. A simple look of love and contrition coming from the depths of our heart and sent up to our crucified Lord is sufficient to express our adoration and our gratitude to Him. It is also an appeal to the Blessed Virgin to intercede with the Heavenly Father for the conversion of sinners.

The efficacy of this devotion is proved by the consoling conversions which it obtains and by the holy deaths which are its fruit. We venture to say that it becomes a source of graces to all those who practice it, for never in vain does one approach Jesus Christ Crucified.

PRAYERS

PRAYER OF
ST. MARGARET MARY

My God, I offer Thee Thy well-beloved Son, in thanksgiving for all the benefits I have received from Thee. I offer Him as my adoration, my petition, my oblation and my resolutions; I offer Him as my love and my all. Receive, O Eternal Father, this offering for whatever Thou willest of me, since I have nothing to offer which is not unworthy of Thee, except Jesus, my Saviour, Whom Thou hast given me with so much love. Amen.

CONSECRATION TO THE
SACRED HEART OF JESUS
(Composed by St. Margaret Mary.)

O Sacred Heart of my Lord and Saviour Jesus Christ, to Thee I consecrate and offer up my person and my life, my actions, trials and sufferings, that my entire being may henceforth only be employed in loving, honoring and glorifying Thee. This is my irrevocable will, to belong entirely to Thee, and to do all for Thy love, renouncing with my whole heart all that can displease Thee.

I take Thee, O Sacred Heart, for the sole object of my love, the protection of my life, the pledge of my salvation, the remedy of my frailty and inconstancy, the reparation for all the defects of my life, and my secure refuge at the hour of my death. Be Thou, O most merciful Heart, my justification before God Thy Father, and screen me from His anger which I have so justly merited. I fear all from my own weakness and malice, and placing my entire confidence in Thee, O Heart of Love, I hope all from Thine infinite goodness. Annihilate in me all that can displease or resist Thee. Imprint Thy pure love so deeply in my heart that I may never forget Thee or be separated from Thee. I beseech Thee through Thine infinite goodness, grant that my name be engraved on Thee, for in this I place all my happiness and all my glory, to live and to die as one of Thy devoted servants. Amen.

(*An indulgence of 3 years once a day; plenary indulgence once a month, on the usual conditions, for daily recitation of this prayer.*)

LITANY OF THE
MOST SACRED HEART OF JESUS
(*For public or private use.*)

Lord, have mercy on us.
  Christ, have mercy on us.

Lord, have mercy on us. Christ, hear us.
Christ, graciously hear us.
God the Father of Heaven,
Have mercy on us.
God the Son, Redeemer of the world,
Have mercy on us.
God the Holy Ghost,
Have mercy on us.
Holy Trinity, One God,
Have mercy on us.

Heart of Jesus, Son of the Eternal Father,
Have mercy on us.
Heart of Jesus, formed by the Holy Ghost in the
womb of the Virgin Mother,
Have mercy on us.
Heart of Jesus, substantially united to the Word
of God, *etc.*
Heart of Jesus, of infinite majesty,
Heart of Jesus, holy Temple of God,
Heart of Jesus, Tabernacle of the
Most High,
Heart of Jesus, House of God and Gate of
Heaven,
Heart of Jesus, burning Furnace of charity,
Heart of Jesus, Vessel of justice and love,
Heart of Jesus, full of goodness and love,
Heart of Jesus, Abyss of all virtues,
Heart of Jesus, most worthy of all praise,
Heart of Jesus, King and center of all hearts,
Heart of Jesus, in Whom are all the treasures of
wisdom and knowledge,

Heart of Jesus, in Whom dwelleth all the fullness
of the Divinity,

Heart of Jesus, in Whom the Father was well
pleased,

Heart of Jesus, of Whose fullness we have all
received,

Heart of Jesus, desire of the everlasting hills,

Heart of Jesus, patient and abounding in mercy,

Heart of Jesus, rich unto all who call upon Thee,

Heart of Jesus, Fountain of life and holiness,

Heart of Jesus, Propitiation for our sins,

Heart of Jesus, filled with reproaches,

Heart of Jesus, bruised for our offences,

Heart of Jesus, made obedient unto death,

Heart of Jesus, pierced with a lance,

Heart of Jesus, Source of all consolation,

Heart of Jesus, our Life and Resurrection,

Heart of Jesus, our Peace and Reconciliation,

Heart of Jesus, Victim for our sins,

Heart of Jesus, Salvation of those who
hope in Thee,

Heart of Jesus, Hope of those who die in Thee,

Heart of Jesus, Delight of all the saints,

Lamb of God, Who takest away the sins
of the world,
   Spare us, O Lord.

Lamb of God, Who takest away the sins
of the world,
   Graciously hear us, O Lord.

Lamb of God, Who takest away the sins
of the world, *Have mercy on us.*

V. Jesus meek and humble of heart,
R. *Make our hearts like unto Thine.*

Let Us Pray

Almighty and eternal God, consider the Heart of Thy well-beloved Son and the praises and satisfaction He offers Thee in the name of sinners; appeased by worthy homage, pardon those who implore Thy mercy, in the name of the same Jesus Christ Thy Son, Who lives and reigns with Thee, world without end. R. *Amen.*

LITANY IN HONOR OF
SAINT MARGARET MARY
(For private use only.)

Lord, have mercy on us.
   Christ, have mercy on us.
Lord, have mercy on us. Christ, hear us.
   Christ, graciously hear us.
God the Father of Heaven,
   Have mercy on us.
God the Son, Redeemer of the world,
   Have mercy on us.
God the Holy Ghost,
   Have mercy on us.
Holy Trinity, one God,
   Have mercy on us.

Holy Mary, Mother of God and Patroness of the Order of the Visitation, *pray for us.*

Saint Margaret Mary, disciple and apostle of the
Heart of Jesus, *pray for us.*

Thou who didst have the Immaculate Virgin for
thy Mother and Mistress, *etc.*

Precious pearl of the Kingdom of Heaven,

Thou who wast associated with the seraphim in
adoring the Heart of Jesus,

Victim and holocaust of the Heart of Jesus,

Privileged adorer of the Heart of Jesus,

Faithful image of the Heart of Jesus,

Thou who, like St. John, didst repose on the
Heart of Jesus,

Pure dove who didst make thy dwelling in the
opening of the Heart of Jesus,

Thou who didst live profoundly hidden in the
Heart of Jesus,

Model of obedience and mortification,

Faithful imitator of the meekness and humility of
the Heart of Jesus,

Violet of the garden of St. Francis de Sales who
didst shed throughout the Church the good
odor of Jesus Christ,

Thou who wast crucified with Christ,

Thou whom the Holy Ghost favored with the gift
of prophecy,

Most wise and gentle instructress of souls called
to the religious life,

Merciful advocate of sinners,

Charitable benefactress of the sick,

Joy of thy holy Order and glory of thy people,

Thou who dost extend thy special protection to
all who are devoted to the Heart of Jesus,

Lamb of God, Who takest away the sins
   of the world,
   Spare us, O Lord.
Lamb of God, Who takest away the sins
   of the world,
   Graciously hear us, O Lord.
Lamb of God, Who takest away the sins
   of the world,
   Have mercy on us.

V. Grace is poured abroad on thy lips.
R. *Therefore God hath blessed thee forever.*

Let Us Pray

O Lord Jesus Christ, Who hast wonderfully
revealed to Saint Margaret Mary the unfathoma-
ble riches of Thy Heart, grant that through her
merits and following her example we may love
Thee in all things and above all things, and may
thus be accounted worthy to obtain an eternal
resting place in Thy Heart, Who livest and reign-
est with the Father and the Holy Ghost, world
without end. R. *Amen.*

PRAYER TO
ST. MARGARET MARY

O St. Margaret Mary, permitted by the Sacred
Heart of Jesus to become partaker of Its divine
treasures, obtain for us, we beseech thee, from
that adorable Heart, the graces that we need. We

ask for them with boundless confidence; may the divine Heart be willing to grant them to us through thine intercession, so that once again It may, through thee, be glorified and loved. Amen.

(300 days Indulgence each time the above prayer is recited piously and with a contrite heart.—Pius XI, June 22, 1922).

If you have enjoyed this book, consider making your next selection from among the following . . .

Prices guaranteed through June 30, 1987.

At your bookdealer or direct from the publisher.

Prices guaranteed through June 30, 1987.